BETWEEN HOURS

BETWEEN HOURS

A Collection of Poems
by Psychoanalysts

Edited by
Salman Akhtar

KARNAC

First published in 2012 by Karnac Books

Karnac Books Ltd
118 Finchley Road
London NW3 5HT

British Library Cataloguing in Publication Data

A C.I.P. for this book is available from the British Library

ISBN: 978-1-78049-064-9

Printed in Great Britain
www.karnacbooks.com

To

The memory of my father and my maternal uncle

JAN NISAR AKHTAR & MAJAZ LUCKNOWI

Giants of 20th Century Urdu Poetry

CONTENTS

ACKNOWLEDGMENTS   ix

PROLOGUE
The poet who became a bridge   xi

POEMS BY TEN PSYCHOANALYSTS
Salman Akhtar   3
Gerald J. Gargiulo   13
Forrest Hamer   23
Sheri Hunt   33
Alice Jones   43
Eugene Mahon   53
Rebecca Meredith   63
Arlene Kramer Richards   73
Arnold Richards   83
Elise Sanders   93

EPILOGUE
The spider who became a poem   103

ACKNOWLEDGMENTS

I am thankful to the colleagues who have contributed to this volume. Their agreement with my insistence that each poem fit on one page was especially touching. The gratitude I feel for the suffusion of poetry in my childhood background is in my blood and needs no words. Due to the input of someone who must remain anonymous, the title of this book was improved. My assistant, Jan Wright, prepared the manuscript with her usual diligence which I greatly appreciate.

The poet who became a bridge

New Jersey is a frequent butt of jokes on late-night television. And, to be sure, it is the home of *Bada-Bing*, the smoke-filled hangout of the television's most loved criminal gang, the *Sopranos*. But, by God, it is also the intellectual cradle that sustained Edison and Einstein, and the locale of the hallowed Princeton University. More to the point of our book here, New Jersey happens to be the motherland of great poets including the exalted Walt Whitman, the celebrated Joyce Kilmer, the witty Dorothy Parker, and, in more recent times, the expansive Allen Ginsberg, the urbane Robert Pinsky, the fiery Amiri Baraka, and the path-breaking Alicia Ostriker. It is also a state where highway rest areas, major buildings, and even bridges are named after poets!

One such structure is the Walt Whitman Bridge, linking Philadelphia to the "Jersey shore". Extending over the Delaware River, its majestic spans connect two distinct cultural territories. On its northern end is Philadelphia, the proud American town where Jefferson labored over the Declaration of Independence, Betsy Ross stitched the national flag, and the country's first hospital opened its doors to ailing citizens. On its southern end are the bedroom communities of New Jersey, family-oriented beach towns, and Atlantic City—the Vegas "wannabe" of the East—with all the required glitter, gaudiness, and gambling establishments. Note, I am not mentioning the Mafia, winos, pimps, or hookers. But what I say or don't say pales in front of the simple fact that only a bridge named after a poet could manage to unite such diverse idioms of life. After all, what is poetry if not a bridge between the sequestered and seemingly irreconcilable chunks and fragments of human experience—sensual, cognitive, spiritual, and absurd.

Poetry links the *unknown and known*. The movement in poetry is "from delight to wisdom" and not vice versa, declares Seamus Heaney. Poetry informs us about the inner state of affairs and enhances empathy with the self. It brings the unconscious out and helps "mentalize" the unspoken substrate of subjectivity. If Freud was correct in declaring that "the repressed exercises a continuous pressure in the direction of consciousness" then poetry is a "de-repressing" medium par excellence. No wonder repressive cultures dislike poetry though they give rise to it in bushels.

Poetry also acts as a bridge between the *preverbal and verbal*. It seeks to vent emotions that "lie too deep for words". This is not to say that ideational content, relational scenarios, and self-based narratives acquired after the non-verbal period of childhood do not contribute to the ultimate text of a poem. Of course they do. However, the near-somatic flicker of sentiment that characterizes poetry seems derived from the preverbal area of infantile experience.

By its emphasis on the prosodic and kindling power of speech, poetry also brings *music and prose* together. Now we know that music (with its origins in the fetal exposure to the placental pulsations and the baby's exposure to the maternal heartbeat, while being held, and to lullabies) have links to the mother's body and prose—viva Lacan—to the law-giving father. By linking music with prose, poetry constructs a bridge between *mother and father* and in this architectural flourish lies the source of its oedipal agony as well as its civilized triumph. At the same time, the fact that words in poetry are used not only for their connotative expanse but also for their prosodic qualities results in poetry's traveling poorly across cultures and languages. Indeed, while great prose has been written in acquired languages (e.g., by Beckett, Ionesco, Nabokov, Rushdie, and Solzhenitsyn), great poetry has never been written in a language other than in the poet's mother tongue.

The bisexual foundation of poetry is also discernable at the societal level. Certain cultures are more welcoming of poetry than others. Those which, in Joseph Brodsky's words, are essentially a "republic of ends and means" regard poetry to be a pastime of troubled adolescents, loners, and the mentally deranged. In contrast, societies based upon communal affiliation and faith, and celebration of rituals, find poetry rewarding. Fundamentally "paternal" (emphasizing instruction, search, autonomy, and mastery of external reality) versus fundamentally "maternal" (valuing emotion, affirmation, soothing and relatedness) nature of culture, insofar as such generalization are possible, lead to over-valuation of prose over poetry, and poetry over prose, respectively. It is also possible that paternal cultures encourage self-dosed physicalization of mental pain via athletics and maternal cultures encourage mentalization of the same pain via reading or writing of poetry.

An optimal blend of *emotion and logic* also characterizes good poetry. Too much of the former renders its misshapen and idiosyncratic. Too much of the latter renders it didactic and sermon-like. Most poems scribbled in journals found in state hospitals belong to the former category. Most poems commissioned for sociopolitical purposes belong to the latter category. Of course the reader's subjectivity plays a role here as well. The realist and the romantic differ in assessing what is "too much" emotion or, for that matter, "too much" logic.

Yet another bridge constructed by poetry is that between feelings of *merger and separation*. Almost all the component devices of poetry (e.g., meter, rhyme, alliteration, simile, metaphor, onomatopoeia, line break) create a sensually gratifying experience by creating fusion between separate entities and linkage between contradictions. Each element of poetry, in its own particular way, evokes a dualism and magically overcomes that very dualism. Acting in unison, the various elements of the poetic form quench the emotional thirst for the sweet milk of relations, bonds, links, and connectedness. Separation and separateness are both recognized and denied.

Simultaneous kindling of *the right and left brain* also accounts for the soothing effects of poetry. Generally, it is one or the other that dominates our experience, even though both hemispheres contribute to it. Poetry, however, is an "equal opportunity employer". The musical and pictorial power of the right brain are enlisted by poetry to cooperate with the linguistic powers of the left; and by the auditory driving effects, the lower levels of the nervous system are stimulated in such a way as to reinforce the cognitive functions of the poem, to kindle the memory of certain experiences, and promote physiological harmony.

Finally, poetry brings *reality and unreality* together. This is why it is not to be questioned. Like games, religious faith, children's laughter, and, yes, love, poetry resides in the "intermediate area of experience". It is not located midway between reality and unreality but simultaneously accommodates both of them. It is both subjective and objective. It breathes in the external world but is hardly tangible. It comes from within but is not a hallucination. The property of both its creator and audience, poetry is a bit like Winnicott's "true self"; the essence of both is incognito.

Pray tell who might grasp this last-mentioned point better than the psychoanalyst? These clinicians of despair take hourly walks on the shores of anguish and triumph, torment and mastery, defilement and virtuosity. So when ten of them pick up the harp themselves and when their sad, yet knowing souls begin to sing, what we get is truly a symphony of insight. We are regaled and informed, stimulated and enlightened. We get a glimpse of the non-clinical corners of the analytic mind, note how poetry and psychoanalysis are related, and witness the creativity of psychoanalysts *Between Hours*.

POEMS BY TEN PSYCHOANALYSTS

SALMAN AKHTAR

Salman Akhtar comes from a family of renowned poets and writers. He is the author of seven collections of poems. Three of these, *The Hidden Knot* (1985), *Conditions* (1993), and *Turned to Light* (1998) contain his poems in the English language and the other four in his native Urdu. He is also a prolific contributor to the psychoanalytic literature, having fifty-six authored or edited books to his credit. A psychiatrist, psychoanalyst, editor, and teacher by profession, Dr Akhtar holds the rank of Professor of Psychiatry at Jefferson Medical College, Philadelphia, PA. He is also a Supervising and Training Analyst at the Psychoanalytic Center of Philadelphia. He lives in suburban Philadelphia with his wife and their beloved dog, Majnun.

Conceptions

A big black cloud
    dropped two smiling raindrops
    in the purple courtyard
of the lotus on a satin lake.
A blue owl
    and a pink mynah
    flew out of the flower.
And the flower undulated with waves of lusty pride.

Rhythm and Union

(On John Ross's and Ann Maloney's Wedding)

When the mundane and the sacred became twins.
When laughter took the form of a tandem bicycle
When imagination became a round vessel,
    round like a fat woman's behind,
    to contain the Heaven's rain.
When recognition became unnecessary
    and we started calling each other by the same name.
When flesh became noble and soul erotic, wet.
When, like Hindu deities, we grew serpentine arms, and
    opened our third eyes.
When lips cropped up all over our torsos
    and our handwriting began to sing.
When love and work cross-dressed and passed for each other.
It was then that we became truly humble.
For we realized that
God had made us one. After all!

Worthless Angels

On this fork in my trail
Who can truly sense my conflict?
Who can show me the right path?
The one who cries with my pain
    does not know
    which way to go.
The one whose counsel is astute
    feels not my longing to take the other route.

Summary

Deprivation precedes greed. Rage follows humiliation. Vanity masks hollowness. Glamour seeks solace. Lust blinds reason. Logic mutes passion. Envy spoils admiration. Pity harbors disgust. Ambition corrupts talent. Surprise implies innocence. Learning acknowledges ignorance. Guilt accompanies gratitude. Humility respects history. Love sustains all.

A World without Seasons

(To the Indian immigrants in the United States)

In the greedy flim-flam
For two worlds, we have lost the one in hand.
And now,
Like the fish who chose to live on a tree,
We writhe in foolish agony,
Our gods reduced to grotesque exhibits
Our poets mute, pace in the empty halls of our
        conversation
The silk of our mother tongue banned from the fabric
Of our dreams.
And now
We hum the national anthem but our
Pockets do not jingle with the coins of patriotism
Barred from wedding and funerals
We wear good clothes to no avail
Proudly we mispronounce our own names
And those of our monuments and our children
Forsaking the grey abodes and sunken graves of
Our ancestors, we have come to live in
A world without seasons.

That Summer

I remember that evening
White wine, supper on the deck
Both kids still in the pool
Honeysuckle in the warm air
I remember
A fearless eye contact with the Doberman across the fence
An absent-minded greeting to its owners
Then turning, noticing the rust on the swings in the
    backyard
Nostalgia, soon afterwards
Missing the vigor of yesteryears
Thoughts about parents, an elementary school event, an old
    girlfriend
I remember
And
I remember, later that night
My body melting in the sweet furnace of your embrace

Our Love

(For Monisha)

There is love that rushes through the staircase of the eyes into the
    vault of heart.
There is love that rises from the groin, like an architect's dream:
    proud and soaring
There is unrequited love that cuts the soul like a knife,
    anguish forced to become sublime by the closed doors of nature.
This is the stuff of poetry.

Then there is love that smells of baby milk
Love which brings caution in a duffle bag
Love which has lost that bag on its way to the heart's threshold
Love of silent animals, love of bearded friends, and love of England
Love that sets two brothers apart
Love that grows like a tree and sings like an autumn night

These loves frolic in the meanderings of the poet,
    flicker through the mutterings of madmen,
    float in the musings of the Israelites, Chinese, and the Hindu.

Once in a while they whisper their secrets into each other's ears.
The music that spreads across the universe then is the sound of the
    cosmos breathing.
And of our love.

Calendar

A page turns
And suddenly what was love
    is simply a "valuable experience" from the past.
You stop pushing the outsides of the envelope,
    stay within,
    feel relieved that the polyp in your throat is benign,
    can be removed easily.
A page turns.
    You need glasses to read.
    Your son leaves for college.
And, suddenly, fall is in the air.

To an Impotent Rescuer of My Soul

I lie on the floor of the ocean.
Wrapped in a green shawl of algae.
My eyes loosened from their sockets
    Float near my navel.
My skin bloated.
My finger nails, hors d'oeuvres for crustaceans.

I lie on the floor of the ocean.
Poemless. Long dead. Gone.
And, you ask me
If I am worried about the rain that is coming tonight?
If I need a raincoat, an umbrella?
How considerate of you.
How thoughtful!

Reflections

The space
Like an empty boat adrift
Is wider
Than a child's dreams
When mother leaves.

And earth
Now turned cold
In its indifference
Holds memories
Hopes
And
make believe.

Immortalized
Those last meals
That last
Touching,
Those newly
Arrived tears.

Who gives such knowledge …
We do not wander
after
death
but, like a forgotten childhood,
It awaits our
memory.

Silent Spells

I am not a maple tree
Japanese in its delicacy
its leaf
five-pointed
diminutive
is innocently green.

From my silence
could I grow that delicately
push out from the jumble of my roots
a sacred pointed leaf
whose dance with the wind
is quite enough for it to be.

A Water Maple vigils nearby
enfolding, like an ancient
cathedral,
the hard-won innocence of the lighter green.

And I …
I am just a mirror
to the scene,
wondering who will catch the image next,
And what it is
that they will see.

Death in the Open

Chartres,
I am convinced, is so silent
So still
Because it holds,
As a grieving mother does,
The prayers of all those centuries.

Silent Lady of the plain
When I saw you
I knew
First view was but a memory
And I have come to tell you,
I have lost a friend,
And forgotten
How to pray.

Un-titled

Love is more than the deed
more than the finding of a hand
in the night.

The seeds of life run deeper
yearning again.

What haunts us most
memory or desire?

Or, are we flames in a great burning,
we cannot know.

Friday Night

Death came last night
In a phone call
    An old man died
    On time.

Do not talk to me
Of love for god
The comforter of pain
And look appalled, when I don't understand.
My father let me know that he was leaving
With just a grasp of hand.

Unburdened
By future dreams
Admist bedpans and IV's
    He grieved the love he had not given
    And I was shriven.

A grey morning dove
Pecks quietly,
Out of sight.
Tears gone,
I ponder the night.

April Thoughts

Gentlest giant
Had
By rain
Laden
Water maple,
Yesterday
I caught
You
Soberly framing
The non-
Existent
Sky.

FORREST HAMER

Forrest Hamer is the author of three books of poetry: *Call & Response* (Alice James Books, 1995), winner of the Beatrice Hawley Award; *Middle Ear* (Roundhouse Press, 2000), winner of the Northern California Book Award; and *Rift* (Four Way Books, 2007.) His work appears in three editions of *Best American Poetry,* and he has taught on the poetry faculty of the Callaloo Creative Writing Workshops. He is a graduate and faculty member at the San Francisco Center for Psychoanalysis, in private practice in Oakland, and a staff member at the Masonic Center for Youth and Families in San Francisco. For years he imagined that his writing life and clinical life existed mostly in parallel but were not related necessarily to each other. But, over time, the two careers developed in tandem, coming closer to each other. He now strives to be more conscious of the fact that the poems he authors are written by a psychoanalyst, and the psychoanalysis he practices is conducted by a poet.

A Poem Also about Healing

How, at the end of a long and complex story,
Something is revealed which changes everything;

How perception is as much what we anticipate
Than what in retrospect we sense;

How, after the years of feeling unwell, he was awakened
Early one morning by the thought, *It's about time now*

To write all of this down; how there was nothing yet
Very important to say, but even in saying this

The long years of thinking there would be no more life
Was only a minute, the ill-begotten past

Merely the beginning of a poem.

Genesis

There are endless poems
in the world,
and each one seeks its listeners out.
A poet hears first some hint,
coaxes this
into the body
where listening begins

between them—the poem
making the poet,
the poet making the poem.
After, each listener becomes another
maker, each time the poem made
all over again, each time
becoming something new.

A Body of Thought

Think of any two people you imagine making
love to each other, and what this loving has to do
with you
Think about the relation between this
and that: one thought and what would be a thought
Think of all those ways It makes one humble
The two of them fumbling with clothes and then
with such frank beauty. O,

Think of thought breaking
into vast lands longing
And think of this creation and all the ways there
are The two of us impelled
towards a moment
oblivious, always, to that which thinks us up.

Lesson

It was 1963 or 4, summer,
and my father was driving our family
from Ft. Hood to North Carolina in our 56 Buick.
We'd been hearing about Klan attacks, and we knew

Mississippi to be more dangerous than usual.
Dark lay hanging from trees the way moss did,
and when it moaned light against the windows
that night, my father pulled off the road to sleep.

                                                    Noises
that usually woke me from rest afraid of monsters
kept my father awake that night, too,
and I lay in the quiet noticing him listen, learning
that he might not be able always to protect us

from everything and the creatures besides;
perhaps not even from the fury suddenly loud
through my body about this trip from Texas
to settle us home before he would go away

to a place no place in the world
he named Viet Nam. A boy needs a father
with him, I kept thinking, fixed against noise
from the dark.

Revision

That girl in middle school we thought was ugly,
Who, nudged by the teacher to show herself,
Sing something, anything, to come out from her shy, hurt life,
Stood in front of the class with her head down, singing,
"I second that emotion."

That we had been boisterous, musky, wild;
That not too long from then some ones of us would disappear;
That each of us had testified
Not knowing what we'd see by being seen;

We saw that girl was several weeks along,

And nothing was the same
Because the same had never been.

Taking Leave

Turning to go, I also know
    I can hear now.

Before I knew this, I would say
    I couldn't,

And what a sorrow that seemed.

Initiation

After I stumbled through the gauntlet, after they had hit me
As hard as they could,
Some there only because there was somebody else
To be brought in, I joined them
In greeting the new ones, the frightened and longing ones,
And I punched as hard and as much as I could, something
Filling in me I would tell you was a thrill
Only because I had no better word for it.
There was another word for it: violence
Made my mother impatient with me, she would call me evil,
And I knew what she was trying to talk to me about—
How much I hated,
How much I wanted and how greedy wanting made me.
What I wanted most were better words.

The Point of the Story

That next morning, a little depressed, I said, Self,
Don't you finally get tired of yourself?
And the answer was obvious, but not absolute,
Which is, of course, just like a self.
So I countered, What's your point?, uncovering

The whole other realm of questions and conjectures,
Only a few of which make sense.
Over dinner, my friend who was writing another novel
Had said she thought the narrative impulse was too much
With us in the end, even when

We move toward fracture, write towards nonsense.
I agreed with her, lamenting that I sometimes feel
I only tell one story,
And there is always that other side.
As for all of the other stories, Well, you can imagine.

A book has its cover, its author
Probably not a good judge. Despite my best efforts,
I keep coming back to talking to myself.
It's harder and harder to finally tell
Just what I'm saying back.

Thirst

I am trying very hard to figure
what happened to my grandfather's well,
the one I can no longer find as I
remember the back yard of his house.

Each day I set myself to notice a color
and how it makes itself in the world.
It is one of the ways I animate attention,
a way to hope. If on a Wednesday

I go looking for yellow, I find it
in the obvious places; then, anywhere, almost
everywhere, so much I must remind myself
there is no yellow, really, but this.

SHERI HUNT

Sheri Hunt is an adult, adolescent and child psychiatrist and psychoanalyst and is certified by the American Psychoanalytic Association. She is on the faculty of the Seattle Psychoanalytic Society and Institute. Her interest in writing and poetry led her to becoming a, editorial board member of *The American Psychoanalyst*. She has been editing its poetry column for over ten years. Dr. Hunt has had numerous publications ranging from medical topics to essays and poetry. Her inspirations include family life, her work, which deeply immerses her in the inner worlds of patients young, middle aged and old, and the mountains, islands and waterways of the Pacific Northwest.

Night Terrors

You look sleep's
Sheer, black glassy drop
Spit in its eye
And jump!

Like crossing a street
When it's not your turn
And you feel air then steel
Whizz neatly by
In a single carbonized gasp.

A night's sweated ice
Wakens you with a yell
Not sure where blankets end
And you begin.

But, it must have been
A helluva fight.

Sunset Rain

Purple mottled sky bruises
Where wet has left sugared marrings
Pulse a wounded inner pink.
Pool towards damp edges
Sweetly, like soft apple flaws,
Ripening to rain.

Explaining Stars

Bending trees
That tilt and lift
The tender sky
With noon-sun bliss.

Leafy spires
That pierce the sky,
The holes they make
Are starry-eyed.

And glow at night
So every thinker
Sees constellations
That blink and glimmer.

Yes, you and I
See starry form
In the blue-eyed sky
That the trees have torn.

Vengeance

Like a bird
That has caught an updraft
Hanging suspended,
Wings out.

Keen eyes search
Timelessly search
Suspend time.

In flowing wind
A slipstream crouches,
Leaving an untouched
Pocket of bird.

One ray
One solar glance
Rockets from its eye.

Pinpoints
Flashing down
Remembering,
And time flows easy again.

A Little Company

Speaking strictly season-wise
Aren't you hanging about
A little north, old sun?
We've had weeks of an Indian summer
So cold you aren't even warming yourself.
Go along now,
You'll miss your vernal equinox.

You lazy winter eye
I've caught you blinking
Your enormous
Avoirdupois all over the sky.
What's that? Going south is for the birds?

Then stay for the holidays.
I'd promise turkey
Or some higher flying relation
And mince pies
As round and golden inside as you,

If you promise not to heat up
Melt the snow
Or get jealous of the midnight borealis
Hanging its Christmas tree lights.
Then just maybe we'll ring in the New Year, too.

Spider

This spider in the corner,
I have watched it all summer.
It's grown leggy, plump and bolder.

I admire its tenacity
But I question its judgement-
Half in and half out of its den.

It could have stayed hidden.
What animal hunger
Or edgy, arachnid curiosity tempts it out?

I don't want to kill it,
After admiring it all summer.
What if it lays eggs?

It might mother
A brood that wants
Run of the whole damn situation.

Diurne the Goddess

A woman vined in green
Sinuous summer girl,
She floats among slender trunks
Rarified, essential.
She's caught mid-flight
In metamorphosis
Undressed by Autumn's alchemy,
She merely blushes red.
Midas' touch
A light caress
As gilt to gold
Or whispers barely heard.
Brazen, golden glance,
She turns and in her turning,
Half the world
Goes down to ice.

ETOH

He toppled down the stairs
A fallen angel
Breathing sweet vapours
Of pain free air.

Risking a sheer drop
To pavement
Waiting hard below
To catch him and break his fall,

His bones, his organs
Crack open his head
Filled with empty, egg-shell dreams,
Like lucent, whipped cream.

An angel
Falling from his alcoholic state of grace,
Tipped halo and clipped wings,
Giving way to gravity.

A lambent form
A creature of air and ice
And dirt
And drink.

Oh, this is a darkened star.
Hard to catch
Hard to wish on
Such a meteoric fall to earth.

Green Lake

We live by a lake,
Not dwell.
When we wake up,
It's already been sending out
It morning scent
Of awakening water.
We'll change by our lake,
Growing more alive.

It stirs itself, first slowly.
The lake, our lake, quickens in the ready sun.
The lake abounds,
Animates itself.
The lake's aroused below the surface,
We can always tell.

It's eager,
Overflows our windowsill,
We laugh
Watching it kindle.
Eagles, turtles, mallards,
Coots common and American.
Sun fish, rare fish,
And scooting geese.

The lake is cool eucalyptus vapor,
We are layers,
In its changing currents,
Such life!
We live by a lake,
We do not dwell.

ALICE JONES

Alice Jones's books are: *The Knot*, which won the Beatrice Hawley Award in 1992, *Extreme Directions* (*The fifty four moves of Tai Chi Sword*), published by Omnidawn Press in 2002, and *Gorgeous Mourning*, published by Apogee Press in 2004. She has also published two chapbooks, *Anatomy* and *Isthmus*. Her poems have appeared in *Ploughshares, Poetry, Boston Review, Colorado Review, Orion, Denver Quarterly, Zyzzyva*, and in anthologies including *Best American Poetry of 1994; Blood and Bone: Poems by Doctors; Appetite: Food as Metaphor, Verse and Universe: Poems about Science*, and *Orpheus and Company: Contemporary Poems on Greek Mythology*. Awards include fellowships from the Bread Loaf Writers Conference and the National Endowment for the Arts, the First Annual Narrative Magazine Poetry Prize, and the Lyric Poetry Award and Robert H. Winner Award from the Poetry Society of America. She practices in Berkeley, CA, and is a Personal and Supervising Analyst at the Psychoanalytic Institute of Northern California and the San Francisco Center for Psychoanalysis.

Sex

If you returned from the center
of earth, your skin would smell
of volcanic ash forever, sulfuric
fumes would bleach your hair, and
children would run away from you too,
as if some forms of knowledge
are older than earth's crust,
floating on its molten bed and

so is pleasure—invisible behind
mud-names, so that plodding, you
can't distinguish smoke from fire,
the barely endured journey from delight.

Circus

Pitching myself into space,
trapeze swing, an arc
through air, that's it:
pairing form and gesture
to find words, not a fall
into the tent's blackness,
not towards the hungry
watchers, but that catch
at the bar—pulled up

into voice—a mating of self
and motion, to embody
their wedding, one line.

Pool

Daylight droops like an eyelid.
I cruise back and forth mindlessly

then, struck as lights go on
by seeing with each breath—

one eye out
and one eye under water

one sees gray, the other
spotlit blue

alternating sides to breathe—
eucalyptus over lights

then palm trees
over same blue light,

the double-layered waters
bay and pool strain apart

rift in vision, floating
in two worlds

more pleasing not to try
to fuse the two

but leave them over/under
being in them.

Fish

Reaching in, you never know
what you'll find—nothing biting,
or some gorgeous unnamed creature
grabbing on to your line. And
more where that came from. The sea
is teeming with fingerlings, unfed
things just waiting for air, growing
gills to breathe far under, briny
wrigglers, fins thin as filament,

glossy and flapping, *feel them*,
rampant in the heart, in the belly,
inside the mind's tidal hold.

Mystery

I looked inside the body for
the primal secret. Maybe tucked
between the spongy lungs, underneath
the clear omentum, beneath silky
layers of dura mater, inside
the pearly capsule of a joint,
within the mortise/tenon lock
of male and female, somewhere
I had not reached into—there
would be the mouth at the center

of the universe. Something grail-like
was the object of my search.

Open

What we have in hand is a bunch of questions. Don't pander to common sense. We're beyond that, not that it's pandemonium we're after; it's just—be Pandora: open the box—there might be hell or the next pandemic, there might be a panda lazily chewing her bamboo, maybe Pindar penning odes (if they had pens then), or the grand panjandrum telling us what's what. Don't push the panic button, just look.

Dream

A train. Its aisle becomes the family
hallway, enters their bedroom.
All that time to come back … *here*,
to find the exit, now a cat door, down
beside their bed. I squeeze myself through.
A pain in my scalp, maybe feeling
the forceps that hauled me out
against my will. In the yard, I lie
bleeding on the grass and feel myself
about to die. *So this is it.* Terribly,

willfully, I enter further into
the world than I have ever been.

Insight

Revelations come in instants, a spurt—
the ball I hammered open
spit something into my eye. Only
that was acid, poison, like knowing
what you aren't supposed to know. Easier
to be sealed over. Beside the Golden Gate,

among the foam flowers blooming,
an old sea lion floated up, eyed us
with a drooped-lid eye, hailed us with one
scarred flipper, rolled bizarrely on his side
and floated down again. Is that how
the mind preserves archaic treasures?

Commute

When the bridge rose up to meet me
I spread my wings like the toll plaza heron,
stretching beyond the familiar

into air that didn't know my name.
Radio Bach unreeled me, tetherless,
seeing the only holding on

is letting go—something ordinary,
like sitting, when that one black fly
buzzed me into the white wall,

there I go, little ape, unhobbled,
I was waltzing into a space
that never held me

because I held on too hard. No
talons now. Soft padding feet
of the mind out on its own reach,

come home I used to say. Even
the throat unchokes, transparent
insect circles—all I ever was—let go.

EUGENE MAHON

Eugene Mahon is a Training and Supervising Analyst at the Columbia Center for Psychoanalytic Training and Research in New York City, where he also has a private practice in adult and child psychoanalysis. He was born in the West of Ireland where the wind accents the human voice with its moaning and the human voice accents the wind in turn with its own music of defiance. This legacy, after a brief detour in Internal Medicine, pointed him inevitably toward psychoanalysis. When he's not writing poetry or plays (on Freud, Shakespeare, Beckett, Bion) he is seriously engaged in the Art and Science of psychoanalysis in all its clinical, theoretical and applied manifestations. He has published many clinical articles on dreams, mourning, memory, play, working through, the dissolution of the Oedipus Complex as well as articles on Shakespeare, Coleridge, The Golden Section, Prejudice, Purgatory. He has published a fable entitled *Rensal the Redbit* (1960) and one of his poems Steeds of Darkness was set to music by the American composer Miriam Gideon.

Legacy

We are ancient Greeks
Once removed
By a mere two dozen centuries.
In the span of a hundred years
A child can spawn
Great grandchildren.
Bend this line of thinking backwards
Many times
And you could meet
Euripides on the street.
Would you recognize him?
Of course.
The dogs that tore him to pieces
Are sleeping
In ancient kennels inside you.

Paranoia

Two-faced dawn leaves the night
And hurries towards morning to deceive
With a smile and a handful of sunlight
And the black ace of evening up her sleeve.

Dream

Beside me a shaking,
A dream shivering,
A piece of the night
Cornered inside you
Like a wounded animal.
I reach in:
Your flesh bars the way.
Shut out
I can feel the thunder
On an ocean
I cannot see or hear.
Only morning
Will bring the halves
Of us together
When words split
The dream in two.

Self Portrait

To catch a likeness like a fish and reel
It home, you have to throw the self away,
Draw the face as cabbage couldn't feel
Art's fingers on its features, a clay
Image of itself, not the live
Flesh and blood conflicted thing it is.
In these waters of illusion dive,
If you would pull a portrait from the abyss.
What makes you sure the self is in the face?
You don't believe that Beauty's in the skin.
Isn't there a depth beneath the lace
A portrait of without that's all within?
Ply your craft and pigment as you will,
There is a self within whose voice is still.

Clockwork

When I jiggled
The pendulum,
Got it going again,
Gravity restored
To its restless swinging,
I had an instant fear
That Time reinstated
Would run circles
Round my face
Not forever.

Cloak and Dagger

I was a child
When Death first
Pushed a silencer
In my ribs
And slowly squeezed the trigger.
I never heard the click
On the released finger.
I have searched
Everywhere,
In every fold of silence
For that sound,
Like a child
At the door
Of the room
He locked the monsters in
Before he went to bed
And tried to sleep.
In the end
And finally out of earshot
I will hear it
When sound
Can no longer reach me.

Luciano

All the winds
That ever blew
A note of music
From the throat
Of ancient cave
Or ocean crevice
And gave loneliness its name
Found their way
Eventual
Into your mouth
To build a song
That made flesh
Shiver in a sound
It always knew
But never heard
'til you pronounced it
For one first and only time.

Suicide

Kick chair,
Jump from ceiling
Neck the rope
That tears
Breath
From bellows of body.
Tomorrow,
Uplifted,
Breathless,
You will have
None of it,
When someone
Cuts you down to size,
Memory
A hang over,
A lost cause,
A rope of broken love
Outside you,
A rope of broken love
Inside you.

Oedipus

Absentminded
On a staircase
Have you ever stepped
On a stair
That was not there
And felt the whole thrust
Of the earth's gravity
Assault the sole
Of your foot
As if you had stepped
On your father's grave
Before he was dead?
Absentminded my foot:
Swollen with pride
You got what
Was coming to you!

REBECCA MEREDITH

Rebecca Meredith is a writer, poet, and graduate of Seattle Psychoanalytic Society and Institute. Although she now lives and has her analytic practice in Seattle, she grew up on the Mississippi Gulf Coast and in New Orleans, and much of her work comes from her affection for its culture and land. Rebecca's poetry and prose has appeared in numerous literary magazines and other publications, and in 2010 she was chosen to be the first Poet Laureate of the city of Redmond, Washington. She has recently published her debut novel, *The Last of the Pascagoula*.

The Widows

Down in Kosciusko, the widow women
hire black men to come out and cut the yard,
and white men to come in and fix the sink.
They smoke cigarettes at twilight on the porch,
another lightning bug amid the closed day lilies.
Inside, the pendulum clocks strike
from walls filled with men's smiling faces
at weddings, graduations, family reunions—
a roll call of the departed, and the simply gone.
And even though they aren't there any more
to take up the lunch box and go to the school bus factory
or out to the tractors and the herds,
their women's gnarled feet slide into the scuffs at 5 a.m.
And they light the first one of the day,
put the coffee and the weather channel on,
look around them and sigh, thinking
they have finally got everything fixed just the way they want it,
and tomorrow will be soon enough
to go out and check the flowers on the Old Man's grave.

Intergenerational Delta Blues

I went down to the Mississippi Delta to watch my father die,
taking the son who'd never seen
the place where my bones grew, where
my heart stopped and started a million times
in love, in hate, in Godforsaken Bible-Belt fear.
We drove the length of it in August
the heat making a little mirage of every rise in the road,
a promise we could never get to.
That's the way it is, I told him,
the radio plays country and evangelicals, and nothing else.
The cell phones don't work at all.
And all you can do is lay yourself on
the delta's dinner table and let the kudzu take you;
let the Drama-Queen southern thunderstorms
cuss you for a Yankee dog
and submit to it until you can run, still living, away
and just let it have the dead.
And just as I was shedding a natural tear
for the dead man that made me
and the living one by my side
who could run away and so would never understand,
we came to the crossroad of 61 and 49
and he grinned my old family grin,
popped a little Son House on the player
And Lord, we lifted over the delta, feelin' alright,
carried together on the broad, unbroken back of the blues.

Survived by His Longtime Companion

It did not mentioned the wedding ring
or the nights curled on the other side
of the bed, for fear of hurting him.

When he cried out in the dark, it wasn't
Mother, Father, Brother, Sister
But Husband, Beloved, My Own.

The obituary, two lives in three inch summation,
reads "survived by his longtime companion"
who, after, believes the term is—how to put it—

relative.

Goose and the Ladies

I remember the milking barn's smell on cool mornings,
the hay and cow pies, the oil from the milking machines,
and how the hose water ran in little gutters
down each side of the long walkway
between the broad middles and bony rumps.
My Uncle Goose called them the Ladies, and treated
each one as if it was their first date,
excusing himself, begging forgiveness
for the antiseptic wash and the cool, sucking tubes.
He needn't have bothered; the Ladies shifted and sighed
like a hundred splay-footed mothers, easing "Yes, child!"
as the night's load lightened.
And if they ever thought about the bulls and the calves
and the knackerman in the end, they didn't show it.
The milking barn was hospital white, the radio on
to the early morning farm report, where they were stars.
Clover stretched just outside the door and over the hill
to the blackwater creek.
The day would be hot, and the live oaks on its bank cool,
and tonight a tall and rangy man would blush once more
before taking the milk they'd spent the day creating—
giving it all they had.
"Yes, child, yes!"

Poetry in the Suburbs

(The reporter asks, "Why would this suburban town need a poet laureate?")

We don't need poetry in the suburbs, here.
We have drive-thru, and take-out, and delivery
and that is plenty.
We have no midnights, where fear grows teeth
and no daylight to pull them; we have burglar alarms.
No ball ever bounces foul here, no hero quails.
We have X-Box.
No mother sits vigil by her child's bed at night,
her chest so tight she hitches her breath
and offers everything she has,
everything she will ever have,
grasping for the words to make the promise
and the strength to say it—"Please."
We don't need poetry here.
No girl's heart peers out from beneath the thorn bush of her
      discontent;
No colt-legged boy wears his like a beacon, or a chain.
We have free parking, and mowed lawns,
And the smell of new paving never leaves the air.
And if the tattered man at the off ramp, holding a sign
"Homeless—Will work—Anything helps—God Bless"
Makes us tremble and look away, we don't need a way to say to him,
"If what I think of you is wrong, I am most humbly sorry,"
Nor a way to go home afterward,
and say to one another, over and over again, like poets do,
how easily it all can be, will be, lost.

@ The Airfield: The Marymoor Radio
Controlled Flight Club

Except for the occasional daughter,
the oddball woman or two,
this is men's country, this celebration
of fuel and strut and patience
and a good visual-spatial IQ.
Abandoning nightly news, twilit baseball radio,
the children's video games with their hollow victories,
these pilots grip their controls with love's own delicacy,
the grace of thumb and forefinger translated
to the joyous fling of a year's hard work
into the low and dangerous sky.
Caught up in the bee-buzz climb, stall, dive and roll,
the touch-and-go, the throat-clutch pull out,
the young dream forward into what they might someday be,
Daedalus' bright boys arcing toward a heaven near enough their
     grasp,
while the old look back to what they were, or never were.
And these comic book dreamers, time travelers,
riders of biplanes and warplanes and sky-punch missiles,
radio flyers, heartstrings not quite captive, not quite free,
leap, and leap, and leap—
while around them crows and swallows work the field
for a supper of kicked up hopper or light-blind moth,
and generations of eagles watch, unmoved,
from another country, half a mile above.

Said

Down where you can buy anything, fish or fowl,
off a truck parked on the side of the road,
they put the new piranha in the swimming pool
while the storm was taking the tank, and the house, and the yard.
They told me so afterward, striking matches, drawing in
salt-soaked tobacco, holding on awhile before letting go.

They told me how the bottle trees moaned
the way women do when they tear their hair,
how wine bottles, Coke bottles, medicine bottles flew
like they'd been jilted-lover-flung, they told me
how sea turtles swam past City Hall, how dogs drowned.

A storm will do things, they said, a man wishes he could do.
A storm will preach a sermon, break your enemy,
piss seawater on the bushes, dam up the rivers with pleasure boats,
make an El Dorado swim down a dirt road on its back.
You got to love a storm like that just a little, between the sobs.

About those man-eating fish, they said,
they're out there somewhere in a nervous bayou
nibbling on nutria pups and heron feet, circling,
waiting for some damfool man or wind to come along and catch
    them up
and make hitch-hikers of them one more time, just passing through
like everything else. The story, true or not,
is the only thing that sticks around.

In a High Window

In a high window across from my window,
a little cat sits, looking down—
an ordinary little cat with a tabby saddle on her back,
white paws tucked beneath her chest.
Eyes and ears intent,
she watches the buses come and go, follows
the cars, the people, the dogs out for twilit walks.
She watches crows commute out of their neighborhoods,
and house sparrows shop in the trees.
Now and then she rises as if to leap,
as if to catch one of these marvels
and bat it across the kitchen floor,
remade into a thing she, captive, understands.
At my window, sipping my tea,
I dream of cool Japanese mountains
and cinnamon groves, and sugar cane, and you.

When Old, Old Women Up and Get the Blues

When old, old women up and get the blues,
they dream a dream that slowly, gently creeps
around their lonely thighs and collar bones—
and when those middle nights deny them sleep
it leaves them, makes them moan and toss and weep.
When old, old women up and get the blues
for fine old men who somehow went away
a dozen years ago last spring or fall,
they grasp at orchids, dusty sweet bouquets
pressed tight between the parchment leaves of books
like lost consignments of their minted youth.
When old, old women up and get the blues,
they miss the weathered hands that stroke and slip
fine-fingered down the alabaster hip,
long-lingered on the cheek and on the lip,
breath whispered in the hollow of the throat,
night sweat from rocking, tender, bone to bone.
What good can anybody ever do
with bitter liniment and chamomile,
with soft-eyed pity, prayer and sleeping pills,
with whispers in the whisper-darkened hall,
with straps and gears and tubes and tears and all—
When old, old women up and get the blues,
they know by heart the names of what they've lost,
that going back is nothing but a dream,
that going on can have a bigger cost.
It's no wonder that old women look confused,
like babies without mothers,
with the blues.

ARLENE KRAMER RICHARDS

Arlene Kramer Richards is a Training and Supervising Analyst, New York Freudian Society; Fellow, Institute for Psychoanalytic Training and Research; member, APsaA and IPA. Author of 7 children's books including *How to Get it Together When Your Parents are Coming Apart* (Random House Children's Books, 1976), and coeditor, *Fantasy Myth and Reality: Essays in Honor of Jacob Arlow* (IUP, 1988) and papers on female sexuality, perversion, and gambling. Dr. Richards is a practicing psychoanalyst and lives in an apartment in Manhattan and a house in Garrison, NY with her husband, the well-known psychoanalyst, Arnold Richards.

Tell Me

Out with it. Why let all that good stuff rattle around in your head?
Circulating through reverberating circuits?
Keep it coming. The foolish along with the pointedly
Accurate.
There, that man sitting beside me on the bus. Old.
He fastens his folded newspaper to his several times re-folded
brown paper bag
With three bronze paper clips.
Having reorganized the books, I'm ready for a girl-scout
rescue mission.
Get any Halloween headed kids around?
I'm ready for a fright.

Retired

Your eyes went first. They pell-melled down
to shut out cries and Gabriel Heatter on the radio.
Your eyes blurred away dreams and dolls and pictures
of your thirteen busy brothers and sisters.
Your skin grew thick. It piled up horn like young
antelope's head bones to butt packing case ropes.
Your taste buds shriveled against the garlic pepper
mixed pickling spice and oily matjes herring.
Your smell grew with not touching your own skin,
not washing, until it shut out all other smells.
All your senses had retired before you did. You
were retired in Poland father, in New York father,
in Fort Lauderdale father.

Sorry

I must hop out after loving
Leaving your bed-warming back,
Bruising your masculine
Pride by moving now.
Don't lemon juice
Acid shock
that I
Sing.
Navel
Orange,
nectarine
sterile,
I pay with delight in orders of words. Blake
knew better, Ann Frank worse than
Texas grapefruit. We do not die.

Post Office

I walk my loneliness, my excuse for a dog,
to the post office.
I turn back.
I will not mail the letter.
I will not know you gone.

Deer Isle

Dawn exposes pink underbellies of western clouds,
I sit alone, awake, only the birds and I
know this day's smoothness.
Creamy sunshine moves the still calm
Penobscot waters of the bay.
I walk our small land.
Evening primrose grins yellow
in the still gentle enough light
Asters spring back as I pass, Berries
offer sweetness.
My love still sleeps.
I dare not wake him.
He sleeps.

Moving Day

Alone in my appraisal,
solitary under black trees,
I set edged at any sorrow,
Proud I cleared barriers of morning purple fallen leaves
away and away.
I scraped soft from roots and rocks,
Past berm, to outcropping
Bedrock under the soft sheet.
To my lonely bedpost freedom,
Licensed, even,
to sell my own real estate
To when and who
I will. To please.

Mer

At 3:30 my nightmare rides me out of bed.
Red blotches flatter black way.
A year-long swamp festers in the salt water tank
my husband neglects to prove/deny his manliness.
I eat all night, agreeing with him
that my sleeplessness is physiological
When I reach 3:30, he will divorce me
Oysters can't be hurried, he says.
The longer they live, the bigger they grow, I say.
Your pearl will come, he says.
But not me, I say.
My nightmare is a seahorse, she cannot gallop on land.
It is my night, the sea.
Only the shore is dangerous.
Fish and I drown at the border.

Halloween

Your ghost ate chocolates and refused to ski.
Mine drank music and wore boots.
Yours loved to shop, to throw furious pots.
Mine finally removed his red toupee.
Our ghosts dance on the shaggy green rug,
between us.
We'll fold their sheets, to and bottom,
to make our bed

My Mother

A black stain oval on the earth.
She stands on the scorch mark
destroying angels, destroying devils,
She has a simple policy, stand in the burn
untouched as morning ironing
left while the coffee boils over on the stove,
while the children cry, while ice boxes drip.
She swoops elegantly through the scald,
Dancing with mah jong tiles swinging in her ear.
look at my dress, my dress, my own self,
look at me standing and bowing and scraping
a violin melody from the radio.
Look at me, look at me, look at me now.

ARNOLD RICHARDS

Editor of the *Journal of the American Psychoanalytic Association* from 1994 to 2003 and before that of *The American Psychoanalyst*, Arnold Richards is a Training and Supervising Analyst at the New York Psychoanalytic Institute. He is a member of the American Psychoanalytic Association and received its Distinguished Contributor Award in 2004. He is a member of the American Psychological Association–Division 39, the New York Psychoanalytic Society and Institute, the New York Freudian Society, the Psychoanalytic Association of New York, the Western New York Psychoanalytic Society, Honorary Member of the American Institute of Psychoanalysis/Karen Horney Clinic and the New Jersey Psychoanalytic Society. He is the former Chairman of the Board of the YIVO Institute for Jewish Research and a current Board member.

Elegy for Muriel

(Muriel Weinstein died two summers ago. She fell off a mountain
in Switzerland, where she loved to climb)

You celebrated your self
and rightly so.
You reveled in your senses,
pampered them with aliment
sonatas and sauces
flavorful.
You tuned your body
sharpened its sensuality
prepared for its adornment,
clothes your advertisement.
You wrote your own
jacket copy
prideful
before your
fall.

A Picture at the Prado

Fiery Night, Regulus light pierces Leo's sky
On earth leaves rustle A lion roars
Teeth gape from open jaws

David's son minds his father's flock
white headed rams and ewes We watch in horror

Do we dare to tame the beast?
Do we rather run and hide?
A story is a tale, one as good as any other
If it works, no matter

Where is truth? God knows
But is God dead?
That puts de cart before the hearse the darkie said
God a she, God a "mere" God is philosophy
Is that the point?
Who cares about the answer?

Philosophy is edified or dead
Both or neither? Deconstructed

There is truth but who knows it?
Philosophers perhaps not dead.

Embedded.

The Troubadour to his Lady

My poems are narrow lined
Short staccato sentences
Assault the senses
Consonants cracks like machine gun fine

your poems are filigree lace lined
entwined like tendrils
soothing senses
sibilant sounds like zephyr wind

my poems are solid grounded without allusion
or artifice
heavy handed
perhaps too precise
foot falls on earth

your poems are porous evocative
dip below the surface then soar
above like whales
dancing in Baja waters

Fire, Earth Air and Water
Aristoliam elements
separate yet all that is matter an us.

Theology is Cosmology or Before the Weighed the Neutrino

Density is critical
    Our fate hangs on one letter
Not alpha but omega.

Weigh the universe
    Find a number.
Weight over space is what it takes
    To stop expansion from going on
    Forever.

More than one back come mass.
    to a bang not a whimper.

Less than one stars are dim
Cosmic soup keeps getting colder

Omega at one
The world goes on
Balanced on its own teater totter

Earth and moon
Stars and sun

God is one
No matter.

Father's Day

My father had a stubble beard
a crippled gait, a sad face, a quiet voice

My father had a troubled life.
Mother died before her time.
Brother struck by Cossack blade.
Father carried the body home.
Sister shot in dark ravine.
A world destroyed, A god that failed.

My father grew old. His hair turned white.
A wrinkled suit wrapped his frame,

He walked home.
Stooped, returned to wife
Bandit waited in darkened hall

Blood unstopped stained the wall.

My father had a troubled life,
a crippled gait, a stubble beard
a sad face, a quiet voice

A tragic fate
And then he died.

Spider

You sleep across
the room.
Content you say
Isn't this what
you always wanted?

I lie awake
in bed
and wait for you.
This isn't what
I always wanted.

A spider spits
a thread
across empty space
programmed to get the prey
it always wanted.

I envy the spider
Why couldn't I
weave my design
And get exactly
what I wanted?

I know how spiders eat.
But how do they mate
I wonder.

Petersburg, Va. 1965

I was the jailor
You were the jailed

We plotted your escape.
Dark night at Southern Depot.
First stop on the underground railway
Route to freedom.

No more chain gang dogs Greyhound
route to freedom.

Missed by a minute or less
Sinking heart, sweaty palms
Who decided you or I Impala
Route to freedom

No more nigger work wife I 95
Route to freedom.

Conquistador

I spoke at my friend's funeral
It is the custom for friends
To speak in celebration of the person
But not too personal with his wife there

List his papers with dates of publication
But not his mistresses and time and place of assignation.
She knew but blamed herself
I couldn't be what he wanted she said before she died.

I spoke his life
Conquistador, like Freud
Experimenter, not like Freud
who couldn't use his hands
and celibate we suppose after forty.

He said he watched his father count the blueing pills
she took and died
and he could never sleep but stayed awake
counting dreams and measuring other things

Fame was not sufficient nocturnal tumescence
put to work with daughter not wife substitutes
Flaunted his dissatisfaction in her face
I never gave him what he wanted
she said before she died

For my much younger sister on the occasion of her birthday

Shall I mark your birthday when you did not mark mine?

We both started in same space but at the wrong time.
I too soon. You too late.
You Sara's gift. I a mistake

Down the same canal. Greeted by the same face
Brought to the same place.
Crowded and cluttered rooms with little view.
Windows covered with damask opaque to leaves and sky
Furniture covered with plastic.
Transparent in pattern shielding texture from the feel of sticky
    fingers
yours and mine.

We both ate In the same kitchen. Sanitas on the walls,
linoleum on the floor
Fox Ubet Chocolate MyT Fine

We shared space and place faced but not time.
I came to love the man who also made us both.
You were taught otherwise.

Who cut our ties of birth?

I am our father's son.

You are our mother's child.

ELISE SANDERS

For Elise Sanders writing poems has been an organic outgrowth of her work as a psychoanalyst. Through poetry she is able to extend language and imagery to access the unconscious and facilitate transformation. She lives in Minnesota where she has had the opportunity to study writing at the Loft Literary Center, and work privately with poet Juliet Patterson. Elise has a private practice in Minneapolis, and is actively involved with the Minnesota Psychoanalytic Society and Institute. Walking her dogs, gardening, and knitting give her a break from all her verbal pursuits!

Central Park

Bellied in
tender luscious baby green
tiny crocus heads nod
neighborly daffodils skirt
lamppost legs
kick

sidewalks ebb and flow
around the boat basin pooling
at the feet of Alice
wondering in the rabbit hole
about the faint young sun
a pinch of breeze
just warm enough to embrace
and hold with anticipation
in strawberry fields forever.

Old House

holder of my delicate dreams, the rooms emptied,
except for echoes of memories in the chambers
a continuous round of families and friends
the windows welcomes a high light
framed by white arches over worn floor boards,
into the bosom of our lives.

If I wander there, my heart beats so heavy I have to lie
down on the hard floor of sorrow.
I let it slip through
my emotional hands with dreams of ever after,

the table is no longer here, its surface sticky with flecks of glitter
and stray sharpie marks bled through a project,
where you accused me of a cruelty which I did not commit, in fact
buy may have, in spirit.
The old red kitchen counter with aluminum edges
was stripped down to a random spoon,
bare except for all that we placed there to stay:
celestial blue bedrooms, wool carpet so soft
bunny balls bloomed between your toes
and the bare strip, where work men had put duct tape
to anchor paper, protect the floor—and pulled up the finish.
such imperfect protections
We have to accept, ever after.

Dancing Tree

The tree stands
cool blue, ever green
a fascination of motion
his center
so still
so strong
a ladder to the sky.

He draws me in
and reminds me of his
pas de deux with snow
last winter when
he invited me
to build a nest
for my shattered heart.

Dream: The Royal Road

Pine needles scatter across sleep's path, patterns
and patterns in the scrub and sand. Whispering
birches share secrets on a summer night. A root trips,
kicking up dust, and the mind sits to chew
conflicted sticks and stones.
Time ebbs space—a conversation hovers
on the shores of Hole in the Day Lake.
The soul surfaces in dreams, shimmies and flips the air.
Catch and release.
Obsession and reality part ways—for an instant
a clear view, moon spreading her cloak
ruffles down the water. Home at last, logic relaxes
on the porch of sleep, knitting, rocking

Memory Now

Crag of a brick house perched
on the edge of her crown,
Dogwood changed her dress:
tantalizing spring with a shimmer of light
from dawn to sunset;
heartbreaker,
she shed her white skirt
for a simple green frock,
but kept her promise to dress up again,
in fall, all decked out in ruby jewels,
a grand farewell
before going to sleep
for winter, when I dreamt
of the hours I spent resting my gaze
in the arms of my beloved.

The Fishers

(For Curt and Karen Swenson)

Steam edges the lake. Sun infiltrates the pines. Against dazzling water a silhouette catches my eye: a big shouldered bird hulks on one slim leg. From its pedestal on the dock, the great blue heron trains its long arched beak on fish swimming below. I might have thought it was a statue; but it stretches one wing, shifts, preens a shagged feather, and lifts a long question into the day. A girl walks out on the next dock. Pale yellow hair spills down her tiny shoulders and hides her face honed in on tackle. She is so quiet, the heron barely glances her way. Instead, it straightens into an elegant vertical toward a low boat. The boat's out board motor trails a gentle wake, sending a v into the lake, round the island. The island, where the loons return every year to nest and make babies, under the hungry eye of the eagle. You tell me about the oriole mother. Depositing her offspring on the railing, she came up to the house for grape jelly, which you had left there (having saved the strawberry jam for Dad, I presume). She bridged the risk to feed her baby bird, so natural and sweet it made you weep. A big boat loaded with fishermen comes from the north brandishing its trolling rods. Clatter. Dock boards call my curious eyes. The childish racket sends the heron around the point, back to the early sky. It was a mother who woke the scene, in pink robe, hair hauled up for the morning bending over her little girl. A fish flops on the end of the child's line against the diamond strings of a net, until they let it go under the coming sun.

A Dream: The Riddle of the Sphinx

My daughter, weeping like a pickle jar, appears
through a steamy August kitchen where grandmothers
are working water, pots, lids.
She offers me an apple in her panties,
or stain. Her first period,
period dotting the *i's* in little
and girl. The field of childhood
is almost played out; I interrupt
her romp and stoop to initiate her hands to work.
We gather stalks of time, bundling them into months;
my faded apron billows,
grain slips through my fingers, caught in pockets, constellating
my boots. And she asks, *when will you die?*
Here we go round the mulberry bush, on the cusp
her childish anxiety,
or desire for my apron, apples,
mirror. She wants to take my place, eat my heart,
incorporate. I know what I cannot tell:
this inheritance will take more than it gives
pain will play it's own games in her limbs.

A Dream: Magic Carpet

A note chimes, a word, a bird, loose
ends all over the place, I grab a thread
to tie it around memory's wrist.
Alleyoop—head under heels. I press air to find myself—
on Grandpa's Persian rug, veering against star clouds.
Here a thousand and one tales out of time.
Tugging the fringe, I ask more of this incipient memory, but
it takes me where it will in this exotic land of symbolic
turns. Intersections, shapeless as a net, multiply words, images,
meaning. An infantile memory plays
peek-a-boo: crawling, rug stippled hands,
Grandpa tosses me through the ceiling's sky until I drop
into history. Sheep is to rug as Grandpa is to me: tightly plied strand,
DNA spiral. Encoded origins of rug: a piece of wool,
a sheep bleating, a blade of grass.
Morning winks, and so I ride
a sheep, or rug straight into linear life—
weaving narratives one stitch at a time

Beyond the Pleasure Principle

In the palace of the unconscious,
she curtsied to language,
it danced her through dreams,
dizzy, metaphors cracked her head open.
At the table of theory she gorged
on concepts and drank blood from the chalice
of her symbolic heart.

She tried on roles
like costumes: crinolines and bodices, sober black
suits and a silk scarf with the moon and the stars.
Viennese godfathers and new world patriarchs
put her to sleep with deep interpretations of all too human
nature. Ancient wild horses rode her silken neck,
hope and pride pulling the chariot
of her desire to know.
She exercised every role in one: princess, whore,
servant, cleaning her own mess again
and again, trying
to think it through to a fixed identity
only to give up the exhausted dream
of becoming queen of her psyche.

She tried to take herself seriously.
It almost worked.
The role almost penetrated reality.

The spider who became a poem

"There is a mirror that has seen my face for the last time" says Jorge Luis Borges in his poem *Limits*. Deceptively self-evident, the statement (and the sentiment contained here) is actually complex and multi-layered. Think about it. If we take Borges literally, we are prone to wonder about the location of this mirror. Did it adorn a wall of our childhood home? Was it a part of a hat-rack in an anglophile neighbor's foyer? Or was it in the bathroom of a lover's apartment? We also seek the reasons for the mirror's inaccessibility. Did it break? Was the house, where this glass servant dutifully reflected what it saw, got sold? Or, have we, for one reason or other, walked away from it forever?

Avoiding such literal translation hardly sets one free. One is chased by the hounds of deeper inquiry. Does the mirror signify mother's eyes, as Lacan, Winnicott, and Kohut would have us believe? Surely one would never see again her primal and identity-imprinting gaze once the race of life has begun and the delusion of self-agency has set in. Or, does the mirror stand for someone else who recognized us in our psychic veracity? And, then there is the "mirroring" function of culture-at-large, including its rituals, climate and vegetation, and little and big animals. I, for one, was deeply held in attention by the eyes of a cat, a cow, and a dog, while I was growing up. Or, was it I who was "mirroring" them? Matters are far from simple, it seems.

But what does all this rumination about poetry have to do with psychotherapy and psychoanalysis? The answer to this question is simple. Or, is it that the first answer that comes to mind is a simple one? Be as it may, the answer involves my telling my students that they must listen to their patient's talk as both prose and poetry. It is only with such dual attention that they would grasp what the patient is trying to convey. Data arising from these two types of attention are different but complementary and corrective for each other. The composite picture thus derived informs one in a manner that using a single listening approach fails to do.

Initially puzzled by such recommendation, the beginning therapists gradually see its power. One proudly tells that when a patient reported having lived a third of his life alone, he knew that this betrayed a tendency to withdraw from attachments (prose) and a "warning" that parts of him might never enter the clinical chamber (poetry). Another is radiant with discovering that a woman's persistent weeping over her cat's death not only implies her grief (prose) but also displays a heart that has long given up on finding fulfilling human relationships (poetry).

A clinical snippet from my own practice (duly disguised for the purposes of confidentiality) fully illustrates this point: Sarah Green, a fifty-five year old librarian, bought a parakeet to keep as a pet as she was coming out of mourning the loss of a significant romantic relationship. The bird, whom she named Dino, diminished her sense of aloneness, gave some order to her life after working hours, and, over time, became her confidante, and the *raison d'etre* to live. She would talk about Dino as if he possessed in-depth subjectivity, moods, and motivations. I avoided the interpretations that doing dot-to-dot psychoanalysis would have readily offered. I let things be. It was all in the spirit of play. Then Dino died, leaving Sarah devastated. Over the subsequent weeks—no, months—she grieved this loss. The earlier loss of the lover also got reactivated. Sessions were filled with wails and tears. Then one day Sarah reported the following incident. She had returned to her apartment after work and was sitting near a window. She caught a glimpse, from the corner of her eye, of a dark, little spider on the window sill. She was taken by the spider's quiet beauty and kept looking at it intently. A thought occurred to her: "Could it be that Dino has reincarnated as a spider and come to see me?" As Sarah related this, she emphatically said that she knows that there is no such thing as reincarnation and that birds do not transform themselves into spiders. She paused and murmured "Who knows? They might." After this, she turned, looked intently at me and said, "You do not think I am crazy, do you?" Guided by an unknown inner prompter, I spontaneously uttered "No, I do not think you are crazy at all. In fact, I think this spider is actually a poem." Sarah broke into a big and knowing grin which, however, lasted but a few seconds. Somber again, even a bit puzzled, she then said, "What do you mean by that?" I responded by saying that I thought she had immediately grasped my meaning but somehow lost that insight and we should be curious about why that happened. But, I added that, if she wanted, I would be glad to explain what I meant (which I was only then beginning to know myself).

Now, I could wax theoretical and explain the nuances of what, in retrospect, emerged as the rationale for my response to Sarah's asking me if I considered her crazy. That would be hardly suitable for this forum. It should suffice to say that my comment equating the spider with a poem was a spontaneous and, dare I say, poetic, way of saying the following. "Don't worry about reality and don't crowd your mind with what I might or might not think. Just let yourself play with the thought your mind has come up with. It is beautiful, expressive, and helps you in some ineffable manner. There is no urgency to 'reduce' the thought (that the bird might have become a spider) into its supposed psychic constituents. This space where you and I are at this moment is fun and imagination can have a full reign here. Let us go on and see where it might lead us." And so on.

105

Such gradual turning of private anguish into a narrative that enlarges what can be thought about and is, at the same time, aesthetically endearing communication underlies the act of creative writing. Note what Freud has to say about the process. "A strong experience in the present awakens in the creative writer a memory of an earlier experience (usually belonging to his childhood) from which there now proceeds a wish which finds its fulfillment in the creative work. The work itself exhibits elements of the recent provoking occasion as well as of the old memory ... . The writer softens the character of his egoistic daydreams by altering and disguising it, and he bribes us by the purely formal—that is, aesthetic—yield of pleasure which he offers us in the presentation of his phantasies."

A similar process is evident in psychotherapeutic work. Both poetry and psychotherapy attempt to transform the unfathomable into accessible, tormenting into pleasurable, hideous into elegant, and private into shared. Both rely upon putting things into words. Both are not slaves of reality. Both enhance self-knowledge. Both have been shown to strengthen associative links between the limbic and frontal parts of the brain that are, respectively, involved in our feeling and thinking capacities. Both illuminate dark corners of mind and lead to the mastery of what hitherto was a subterranean madness. It is only a slight exaggeration to say that poetry is a one-man therapy and psychotherapy is two-person poetry.

In the end it is all about transformation through listening. Writing poetry requires listening to one's own self and conducting psychotherapy requires listening to the Other. Both endeavors transport the inner and incomprehensible baggage of the heart to the outer and comprehensible platform of the mind. When the effort succeeds, all involved parties benefit. When it fails, there is agony and shame. And, at such a moment, one is reminded of Pablo Neruda's line "What is sadder than a train stopped in rain?"